you used to live here

Journaling in poetry

gold mike-odenigbo

"This emptied place was once home and you used to live here"

For Mother Mary – an expert at loving well and suffering well

Contents

Introduction

Some of the best people I know didn't know they loved or even liked poetry until they tried it for size and realized that it could be different from what they thought. Poetry, like flowers, is a myriad of endless colors, forms, and arrangements.

If you let it, poetry can prime you for hard times. So much so that when you are in the thick of it, it might become a reflex to find poetry in all the plain places it likes to hide—*"... on a store shelf", "...on the glass console", "in a bottle of dye,"*.... And like every other worthwhile thing, poetry demands something of you.

Sometimes, it asks to be peeled slowly, carefully. Sometimes, it asks to be read out loud. It is always to be reread—maybe once, maybe until you cannot forget it if you try. But why try silly things?

If you let it, poetry can give you home when you are tired of being so strong. It can call forth the twenty-one-year-old buried in the tomb that time can build and builds too often. And once again, beauty stops time. Your eyes—filled to the brim with longing and daydreams—might sparkle and water. You feel something you forgot you knew how to feel.

Maybe it's hope.

You Used to Live Here is a collection of thirty poems written over eighteen years. They are in free verse and without a rhyme scheme because I cannot write a genuine rhyming poem to save my life—I tried. I had forgotten about some of these poems until my sister, Trinitas, brought me my old scrapbook from Nigeria. And it showed me my teenage to early twenties self—ridden with angst and brimming with hope at the same time.

Somehow, while moving and living in different places, I forgot much of myself.

This book is an arrangement of sorts—some blooms, some withered. It is something of a journal, reflecting the different moods '*of all the terrible, great and silly girls*' I have been. In some places, it is a projection of my perceptions on people I encountered for only a handful of moments.

You will find the snappy alongside the elaborate. For instance, *Pharisee* is only seven lines long while *Pain* is several paragraphs of prose poetry. As with *Stay*, some poems take liberties with grammar for effect.

I have added little notes to the start of each poem to make them more relatable. But if it works better, forget the notes and decide the context.

You Used to Live Here is divided into two parts:

Part 1: The Citrine House on Sixth Avenue

The first part of this collection is made up of poems I wrote towards the end of my childhood and the start of my adulthood.

Most of my childhood was spent in a cookie-cutter, two-storey, citrine house on Sixth Avenue in Trans-Ekulu, Enugu. Inside, it had terrazzo floors downstairs and red-and-black plastic tiles upstairs. The yard seemed huge, with greenery everywhere—Ixora bushes circling an almond tree, a tall coconut tree standing adjacent, and a pair of orange trees in the backyard holding hands. And we had two rusty tanks that we would climb to get to the oranges.

Recently, my friend Oge, whose family moved in next door when we were teenagers, sent me a picture of the citrine house on Sixth Avenue. And it looked different—shrunken, paint peeling. But the black gate with its spiked ends and rusty circle etchings was the same. The balcony still sat atop the garage. This was the same place where almost all the people I lost in my childhood were once alive and happy in —the same place where there was bright shining morning before a drawn-out night ensued.

My great-grandmother, *Udu'nwagu,* would crack open

icheku pods for my siblings and me. My distant relative, Uncle Jude, lived with us briefly when he was a teenager. They both died when I was five. Ogechi, my mother's cousin, was eight and vacationing with my family when she died in a hit-and-run accident; I was seven. When I was eight, leukemia and botched surgeries killed my six-year-old sister, Tochukwu, my only sister at the time.

We moved to Kano for a while after Tochukwu's death, but we still came back, now and again, to the citrine house on Sixth Avenue. In Kano, I met John and we spent many evenings and weekends playing hide-and-seek with my siblings and his cousins. When John and I were ten, he went missing and was found dead after a few days—discarded, belly cut open and without intestines.

We lost my grandfather, Pa Godwin Okwesili, when I was fifteen; he spent the last twenty-two years of his life bedridden. One of my favorite uncles, Rev. Godwin "Goddy" Okwesili, was shot and killed in his home, a parsonage, when I was sixteen.

At eighteen, I lost the most remarkable person I know, my father, Mike Odenigbo. And right before I turned nineteen, my grandmother, Eunice—who lived with us and who had started dying in installments when my Uncle Goddy died—died.

But in all that night, there were always beautiful stars and a bright shining full moon. There were family and friends that became family. My sister, Trinitas, was born one and half years after Tochukwu died.

There were long road trips back and forth to Kano and short trips to Eke. Oh—the freshly tapped palm wine in Benue, the creepy face of Zuma Rock, the savory steaming hot *okpa* of Ninth Mile!

There was WWF on Saturday mornings. There were Christmases in brand-new church clothes, loud bangers and terrifying masqueraders in the streets. There was Carmelite and the Passion Play on Good Friday. There was the music of Tracy Chapman, Baba Fryo, Don Williams, Patty Obasi, and Mike Ejeagha.... There was Michael Jackson. There were birthday parties, Easters, and *The Sound of Music*. There was unrequited love and romanticizing sadness. There was rooting for Chelsea F.C. because I wanted to be like my big brother.

There was light, and the things I didn't lose numbered more than the things I lost, even though I rarely had the patience to count.

I have tried (failed some, won some) to leave the poems I wrote at the end of my childhood true to how they had been written, true to my younger self.

Part 2: The Red Lion on Whyte Ave

The second part of this collection features poems I have written from my mid-twenties to the present day. These poems attempt to capture the essence of some of the things that cause children to melt into adults.

The Red Lion is a three-storey apartment building on Whyte Ave, Edmonton. It has white-washed aluminum siding, and it used to have a red awning that announced it. This was my first home when I moved to Edmonton as a newlywed. The entrance was two sets of glass doors that encased a buzzer. Inside, the hallway floors and staircase were washed blue-and-grey rug. Our apartment was on the second floor and seemed smaller than it was.

The Red Lion was built in the 1960s, and its kitchen and dining area were thankfully separated from the living room. Its balcony overlooked the apartment's parking lot and the seedy back alley, which was the setting of many crazy stories. But you could also see the neighbors' vegetable garden, framed by their 100-year-old storybook house.

I made most of my Edmonton friends when I lived in the Red Lion. I started my first Canadian job and had my first baby while living there.

There was something free-spirited and chaotic about Whyte Ave. We were only one bus away from downtown and within walking distance of bars, stores, coffee shops, ice-cream places, restaurants, and even The Fringe in August. And it managed not to be too noisy. We slept through the night when a drunk driver crashed into The Red Lion, surviving but killing his passenger, shattering the glass entrance doors, and bringing down the red awning.

I no longer live there, but I sometimes drive past The Red Lion, and it still hints of beginnings. Beginnings of certain things that have since withered away, things I forget to remember for long periods. Beginnings of other things that are so beautiful they cannot end.

And I know the things I cannot lose still number more than the things I have lost, even when it's foggy and hard to count.

Gold Mike-Odenigbo
Edmonton, Alberta

Part 1:

The Citrine House on Sixth Avenue

Outskirts of my Stepmother State

December 2010. For my national service year, I lived in Yola, Adamawa. It was scary, inspiring, different, and treacherous—just like a folktale stepmother.
I wrote this on a bus between Yola and Gombe on my way home for Christmas.

Green smoky mountains
Frame mud and thatch
With the electricity of starry runaway skies
Magic of overriding rocks
And grandmama's million moon musings
Who needs Edison's invention?

Who needs the news?
What more danger than
A cruel cruel sun and few June rains
Dying livestock and greens?
What more horror than
Death cuddling a parent?

If you have a lover
There'll be excuses for your mother
There'll be riverside for footprints

There'll be wagging tongues and angry daddies
And a martyr's gratification
Who needs cellphones?

Yesterday, I saw you
Ebony fine belly
Free eyes mirroring mountains
You and your daddy's sheep
Chatting away

Stay

Grammar has nothing on pettiness, so forget the rules of grammar for a second or thirty.

May 2009. I don't remember exactly why or for whom I wrote this poem. It is interesting how people or stories that were once so important to us can be forgotten. It's interesting how sometimes, something toxic is at least something—seemingly better than nothing.

You won't be blame
If you lie to me
Me, I never tell you
One single truth—not one

It'll mean nothing
If you hate me
You, you disgust me
Thinking you bile-bitters my mouth
But how can you know?

And if you say me
One more time—'I love you'
One more time, I'll blush
Not because you fool me
But to fool you

But please stay with me

Erotic Fatigue

August 2009. 4 parts, in the throes of unrequited 'love'.

I

The stars scatter
Leaving lonely
One sickle moon

Today has died

Power drunk
Power Holding*
Pass the "guilty sentence"

Today has died

Diaries of thinking
Stampede up Memory Lane

II

Once
The sun lived
In your eyes
And your croaky baritone
Was full moon

I was young

Then
Laughter came easy
I was ready
To lick your blood
Since you were sure
My blood was sugar

I was young

III

Just today
Age crept in on me
Like a trade fair pick-pocket

Stealing soul
Killing me-and-you

Now I watch
Darkness deepen

Stealing soul
Killing me-and-you

V

Tomorrow
Maybe, just maybe
Me-and-you
Alive
Will grow young
Hands in hands
We'll *kpapankolo***
This vicious circle
Again

**Power Holding Company of Nigeria*
***kpakpankolo is a children's game played holding hands in a circle and similar to 'Ring-a-ring-a roses'*

Ex

Circa 2010. I didn't yet have an ex when I wrote this, but my friend did, and he was tall and easy to look at.

You, tall glass of palm wine
Fresh and frothing
You raise me high
Then you sashay away
Like the end
Of a dancehall classic

Your eyes, deep potholes
Empty and full
Were they where she fell?
Like I fell
Did she forget her name?

There is a boy with your face
Everywhere I go
I keep running away
From him

Home

Circa 2010. Wondering what my daddy would think after I moved out.

Daddy, can you see
Me now—
Flirty, skinny, smoky eyes, jeans
I know some boys would
But Daddy,
Would you still call me beauty-full?

Do you see the hours I give the shadows?
Happy lyrics I try to mind
Do you see the seconds I give to Jesus?

See my high high heels
Do you worry
Like you worry
I'll fall down
Or can you see
I'm felled, sir

Daddy, can you see
Me now
Would you ask God to
Let me-and-you
And you
Go back home?

Twenty Years

Circa 2009. Inspired by a long married couple and the passive aggression familiarity can breed alongside love and things like that.

He'll buy The Vanguard today
Even though he reads only The Sun
But I won't say 'Thank you'
Because
Again he'll lick his fingers
After my *Egusi* soup
And nod his block head in silence
And if I dare ask if it is good
He'll nod his block head in silence

Yesterday I saw
Traces of grey
On the hair of his balding head
I wonder if he's seen it too
If he'll come back with a bottle of dye too
To die the years
These twenty years

And I'll slip into bed beside him again
Listen to his snoring
And pray sleep on Rosary beads

Volcanic

October 2008. When I wrote this, we had just marked the first anniversary of my father's death, and my grandmother, Eunice, had been dead for 7 months.

The rock s p l i t s
And lava burns
Swiftly down
Pimpled plains
And the air is filled
With infectious grim
Now and again
When Reality comes riding by

Reminiscing (Him and Me)

January 2009. Stuck in traffic on a bus around Ogbete Main Market.

In the purgatory of January's sun
He sits in his gutter
Waiting for nothing
He thinks breathing air
Is enough
So he shouts praises and thanks
To God
God in perfect heaven

Me,
I sit in the bottleneck traffic
Asking God rhetorical questions
Waiting to walk on gaseous waters

Him and me
Our eyes collide
He smiles me one decayed smile
From his decayed mouth
And for a moment
I wonder
The torture of such kiss
If it could ever be

Beguiled

September 2008. Of the dashing of a people's highly raised hopes.

The gates are thrown open
Fate's handiwork
And we race
Like Jephthah's dead daughter
Tambourines
Clanging, and clasping
Our waterloo

Moonwalk

June 2009. When Michael Jackson died.

Beneath the shade
Of this full June moon
I walk
Backwards
Via Memory Lane
To The Place

The Place
The crescent-mooned place
Where Reason died
Where Logic was castrated
There
An altar was built
Where truth and lies were
Burnt together—
Incense
Sanctifying the unholy media
Suffocating us

But we survive
You in heaven
Me in today
Both of us
Miles and miles away from
The Place
The crescent-mooned place
Where lonesome legends live

Untitled

Feb 2010. Unable to sleep at the unexpected unravelling of an online thing that held specs of promise.

One muse dies
Silent *hahahas* resound
Somewhere
Somewhere *QUERTY*
Someone stupid
Finds a song

I'll snatch hours
I'll think of me
When darkness returns
To hold me
To watch me watch
And fight malaria

Adamma

November 2008. When you are no competition for the colorful competition.

Pendulum hips
With the green rhythm
Of the drum

Rainbow, rainbow
Her bitter vow
To eclipse me

Blood lips,
The vampire boasts
Of her conquest!

Now he forgets
The unforgettable forever
Of his youth

And I
Sit in Sahara
Counting sand

It's Fights

I wrote this in May 2006 for Tochukwu, my sister, constant sparring partner, patron saint.

It's fights
It's the memory of you
Fresh morning dew
Playing, shouting, vying
For mommy's attention

It's fights
It's the memory of you
Just yesterday
Biting, plotting, struggling
For rights we could share

It's tears
It's your cold body
Still in death's slumber
Crying, mourning, wailing
Never understood I love you so

Skygazing

September 2008. Watching the day break.

I watched
Her two-minute labour
At the gate of black heaven
Circle light at its threshold

I saw
Selfless self immolation
The last end
Of her 24-hour life

See!
Her azure offspring
Her death, her life

Part 2:
The Red Lion on Whyte Ave

Cocaine's

Circa 2014. At the start of our relationship, I would call my boyfriend Cocaine, and he would call me Nicotine.

Let's melt
My chores are done
I got my headache
From my Lagos

From blasting horns and songs
My passion has grown
Tall like Bimpe's son
Deep fatal stab

Home is your foolish laughing
Stone promises
Of my daydreams

In Thanksgiving

June 2021. The Bombay Company, a furniture retailer, used to have a location at South Common, Edmonton.

Here here
This wilting bouquet
Of thanksgiving
If love was water
Or loamy soil
They would be rainbow blooms
In a vase
On that glass console we bought
From *Bombay*

Pharisee

December 2022.

"It's not what you say, but how you say it!"

- Mae West

One sleek *Sorry*
S t r e t c h e d and pressed
And twisted
To a halo
For your own head

Ashes and sackcloth
Are for simple people

Let Me

Summer 2017. Pregnant on a bus in Edmonton and scrolling Facebook.

What good is your broken heart when
I can't help you hunt its pieces?

And the poetry of your soul—
What does it matter in your soul
Away from your lips?

Someone should have told you young—
All that hair is no good
If it'll live forever in wigs and weaves
And when it greys, will you find grey weaves or dye it?

What stories can your buried accent tell?
Or forget to tell?
Is there a mother faraway that daren't call you hers?

And stranger, what is this friendship of *Likes*?
I forget your name.

Midsummer Gloom

July 2021. The first summer after my divorce, I took a lot of long walks by myself, partly to avoid eating too much loneliness.

I, whitewashed
With the gods I mould
In my image
The gods that summon me at will
That toss me up and down
That break my broken heart

I try to look my prettiest
On the hardest days
I redden my dried-out lips
And try on three pairs of identical jeans
Until it is too late
To walk long alone
In summery suburbs
Face to face
With lovers and their patios

Since you love and want me, Lord
Don't knock and wait—
I'm but a fool
Summon me

You

(The Poem Formerly Titled 'Happy Birthday')

When I posted this poem (formerly titled 'Happy Birthday') a month or so after my 30th birthday, I started getting birthday greetings. I didn't mind the greetings, but I also changed the title.

Today is the morning
When you see
You
When after something like
Thirty years
You see the bitch growing out
Of stacks
        and
        stacks
Of the terrible, great, silly
Girls you've been
Maybe now
You see
You are no better
Than all other God's children
And gods' children

Swimming, choking
Drowning in ponds of mud
You choose and dig and
Keep watered
Throwing, shattering hearts
And picking pieces
To mend, throw, shatter
Repeat

Today is the morning
When you see
You
When after something like
Thirty years
You see that time and cracks
Can be everything
You thought they weren't
Maybe now
You see
You are no better
Than all other God's children

I know

December 2021. When anger fights off sleep.

I know the feeling
Anger boiling blood
Steaming ripples on my skin
A scream escapes my gut
And speeds reckless to my quivering lips
Frightening even me

I know the ghosts
Tucked in the insomniac's pillow
Working too hard
To sieve and swallow sleep
Leaving tired

Tomorrow will be long
But there'll be coffee black

I Think of You

Christmastime, 2020. Of memories glued to big and little things.

I think of you
And when I want to be done
Thinking all these thoughts of you
Our child smiles
A silly song starts
My eyes catch
White hot chocolate on a store shelf

I think of you
I pray God take my heart
And give me another heart
One that can wish you
Love
Light
Flowery things like that
But He won't

I hope you call out my name
While loving her

For Nkiru (1977 – 2018)

October 2018. Nkiru was strong and beautiful and didn't have an easy life. I never got to meet her in person.

You're not somebody's jewel
You're not something only beautiful
With a million and one replicas
Something to be pawned
When something is to be pawned

You're story book woman
I know it and since the first time
I saw you with my ears
Someone to be loved fiercely
Or let alone

You're saffron
And select tastebuds know
You shouldn't die in such hurry

In Remembering

January 2024. It's interesting how two people may remember the same thing differently or how one person remembers something others could swear never happened. Living with my sister again for the first time in 12 years unlocks so many memories.

I tell you my name
Again, and again
You knit your brow
You say you're sorry
You don't remember

Maybe you
You lost your way
Wrecked by siren song
Again, and again
Home is a place
You don't remember

Maybe me
I lost my way
On your trail
Again, and perhaps
Home is a place
Only in remembering

Nakedness

Lent of 2020. Before a crucifix.

True love is the naked rabbi
Bleeding out for
A scoffing people who
Forget nakedness

Long ago, these same naked nailed hands
Stitched together covers for
The scoffing pair that bore
A scoffing clothed people who
Forget nakedness

Pain

Circa 2016. Watching a new widower at his wife's wake and wondering what he must be going through. She was a young mother who died suddenly on her morning run.

Pain starts with your face—it contorts it (maybe a bit, maybe a lot), so that those that have to look at you are worried.
Sometimes, it bleeds and stains those other faces.
Then it goes down to your heart—ceramic and tried—and shatters it. You cannot find most of the pieces, nay bother to reassemble it. Good thing, hearts regenerate so pick the few pieces you can find and keep.
Pain gets to your gut and puts a hole in it. That gut that has held you up, strong, through the years is now pain's plaything and you are terrified of tomorrow.
On some mornings, you wake up happy, forgetting for a moment that she will never come home. Then you remember and curse God all over again for letting pain find you. You apologize to him, and in the next instant, you start asking him rudely rhetorical questions all over again.
You forget all the times she was impossible and remember all the times you were impossible.
Some mornings are just an extension of your nights, nothing different.
Words fail you, especially when you need them most, so you leave

it to others to eulogize her. And they tell little stories that sting hard. They use grand words that anger you.

They cry, and their crying intensifies your anger, so you leave. You mustn't explode, at least not today.

True empathy is impossible and you know it, but you have to listen to the people that try to console you.

Time will come and regrow your heart and heal your gut and give cheer back to your face.

But pain, this type of pain, does not go. It carves a tiny home in a corner of your heart, of your gut. Eventually, you will learn to live your new normal where pain and happy melt and meld.

You will live a good life like she wanted.

And if you had to do it again

August 2024. Of hard conversations that will never be had.

And if you had to do it again
It won't be me
I, a lurking owl
Stuck a hooting
Do you think I had peace
And didn't give you any?

Do you think I found me
But chose shadows?
Just to draw shallow breaths
Swallow storms
Keep pristine our eggshell carpet

It's easy to muddy what was
To say I glossed lipstick
On sharp beak
But what if
Hurt sharpens soft things?

Being Her

May 2024. You cannot control the stories people tell of you, even when you give them words to use.

It's OK to pick words
From stories I gave you
Move them around
Wrench me into an airhead
In a picture
Framed
Hang me high
Everyone can laugh

I'll laugh too
At the airhead in a picture
Framed
Since I stopped
Being her

For Daddy

October 2024. Thinking of how lucky I am that my father has managed to stay alive in my mother and siblings.

And I want to gather all the scraps you left
Paint the sky eternal summer
Tell everyone
Your hair was full and soft
Just like your heart
Your smile, easy and keen
And all the love that lived in your bulging eyes
Caused you to stop needing glasses in time

Even though you have been gone
I never have to live without you

Oh Baby

August 2024. For my babies.

I'd pluck you stars
If you ask nicely
If they mend hearts
If I were tall enough
If they weren't already your eyes
Oh
If your face isn't the full moon
If you don't beam bright
How could I step over these hollows
That litter the night?
Oh
Promise
You'll dance to your own *opi**
You'll never forget you

**opi: Igbo for flute*

Acknowledgements

God has extravagantly decorated my life with amazing people, and I am grateful to Him for them—and for much more.

My children, Somayina and Onaedo, allow me to live out one of my oldest dreams daily.

My parents, Christie and Mike, have always provided for me, supported me and loved me unconditionally.

My intelligent and generous siblings and friends—Obi, Emeka, Ugo, Trinitas, Yakayaka and Jenni—read my drafts and held my hand throughout the process of bringing this book to life.

Obi spent time editing and discussing different aspects of this work. He saw and pointed out my blind spots so constructively, so kindly.

Trinitas treats me as she would herself. She lost sleep reading and rereading various drafts, and advising me on multiple aspects of this work.

Emeka and Ugo allowed me to hear my poems in different voices by recording readings of them.

Yakayaka gave me a blurb and my cover design. He edited the final draft and helps me see things differently.

Jenni spent hours advising me and sharing resources.

She is a talented artist, and her drawing of the citrine house on Sixth Avenue is on page 1.

There are others, too numerous to mention, who take the time to read my writings and who have been so gracious to me.

And there are those who opted into my life, even when it was easier not to, and who hold me in their prayers and words of encouragement.

www.ingramcontent.com/pod-product-compliance
Lightning Source LLC
La Vergne TN
LVHW090138160826
845673LV00017B/2510
9781069132000